THE
TWO TERM
PRESIDENT

James Leon Bryant Jr.

The Two Term President by James Leon Bryant Jr.

This book is written to provide information and motivation to readers. Its purpose is not to render any type of psychological, legal, or professional advice of any kind. The content is the sole opinion and expression of the author, and not necessarily that of the publisher.

Copyright © 2020 by James Leon Bryant Jr.

All rights reserved. No part of this book may be reproduced, transmitted, or distributed in any form by any means, including, but not limited to, recording, photocopying, or taking screenshots of parts of the book, without prior written permission from the author or the publisher. Brief quotations for noncommercial purposes, such as book reviews, permitted by Fair Use of the U.S. Copyright Law, are allowed without written permissions, as long as such quotations do not cause damage to the book's commercial value.

ISBN: 978-1-952822-97-1 (Paperback)
ISBN: 978-1-952822-96-4 (Digital)

Library of Congress Control Number: 2020939814

Printed in the United States of America.

CONTENTS

THE TWO TERM PRESIDENT..................... 1

REASON FOR WRITING THIS TEXT............... 5

INTRODUCTION OF OUR TWO TERM PRESIDENT.... 11

SECOND TERM PRESIDENT SPURS HATE
AND RESENTMENT............................ 15

TRUTH ABOUT OUR POLITICAL SYSTEM.......... 19

EDUCATED FOR THE FUTURE................... 23

WARS GOBBLE-UP OUR FINANCES............... 27

COMMUNITIES, FAMILIES, CHURCHES, SCHOOLS.. 31

BUYING OUR POLITICAL LEADERS.............. 35

VETERANS AND THE DISABLE.................. 39

TRUTH BEING REVEALED...................... 43

PRESIDENT AND THE RIGHT COURSE............ 47

FEDERAL GOVERNMENT TO OVER-SEE STATES..... 51

WHY THE REPUBLICANS ARE CALLED OBSTRUCTIONISTS	55
PROBLEM SOLVING IS OUR BUSINESS	59
TWO SIDES TO EVERY STORY	63
PRESIDENT FOR ALL THE PEOPLE	67
RESPONSIBILITIES OF THE LESS FORTUNATE	71
THINGS ARE SLOW BUT CHANGING	75
EXPOSING EVIL, AND WORKING FOR A BETTER TOMORROW	79
GRADING OF OUR FIRST BLACK PRESIDENT	83
LEADERSHIP THAT FEARS GOD, AND BE LEAD BY HIS HOLY SPIRIT	87
A GREAT COUNTRY TO LIVE IN	91
RESCUING A FALLING COUNTRY	95
SATAN USING OUR YOUNG PEOPLE FOR EVIL	99
INNOCENT PEOPLE ARE USUALLY THE VICTIMS	103
CORRUPTION FROM WITHIN OUR LEADERSHIP	107
CHANGES THAT CANNOT BE STOPPED	111
GIVING IN TO BIG COOPERATIONS AND POWER	115
TRUTH WILL EMERGE AND SET US FREE	119
INDEXES	123
AUTHOR'S BIOGRAPHY	127

THE TWO TERM PRESIDENT

AUTHOR: James Leon Bryant Jr.

TEXTS WRITTEN: The Long Journey, The Long Journey Continues, A Man's Glory, Power of Love, Words from a Christian Mother, and A Father's Love, all off these texts were written to try to tell a true story of how these people live affected me in how I live. The Long Journey Text, tells how I, the author, lived under the "Jim Crow Laws" in a southern city and born to a share-cropper living in a plantation owned house.

A second text that was written; told of how the farming and harvesting of crops that we planted, survival during the cold winter months, sheltering the family from terrible storms, helping our grandparents with harvesting their crops, meeting other relatives from far-away places, and the enjoyment of being around all the farm animals, the fowls and other pertinent things on the farm. Title: The Long Journey Continues; continuation of my journey through life.

Third text written; A man's Glory, this text tells of the help-mate that he chose to be with or the mate that he chooses to be with for the rest of his life, A wife and her duty in marriage, a mother and her duty to her children and unto her husband. Man and woman were created for Glorification unto God. Man's responsibility unto his wife and children.

Fourth text; Words From a Christian Mother, this text tells of the Christian teaching of a dedicated Christian Woman, a caring woman for her husband and her children, love for all people, a woman that trusted in the Holy Bible for all of her decisions and a guide in

Living a Christian life and teaching her family how to become dedicated believers in God.

Fifth text; A Father's Love, this text tells of the love that a father has for his family, his concern for his wife's happiness, being the breadwinner in the family, making rules and policies in agreement with his spouse, seeking spiritual guidance from God and living the life that is taught to his family, seeking God's directions in making rules and setting policies.

Sixth text; The Power Of Love, this text tells the power of love for everyone and everything that God has created, power of overcoming the evil that we experience each day.

In our lives, loving people of all races, all religions, all nations and all that God has created, being good stewards over things that we are blessed to have, our country and the foods that we eat, land to grow our foods, water for both, animal and fowl to drink from.

Seventh text; Our Two Term President, this text tells of the first Black President that we have had, many obstacles that he confronted in trying to get things passed through an un-cooperative Congress lies that were told, disrespectful words that were said to him, strength, prayers and a nation that was seeking change, first four years in Presidential Office was a trial period for the New President, the second term he is determined to get things passed that he could not do in his first four years. Obstructionist in his way, a determined man that has a vision for the nation soon gained the trust of most people.

REASON FOR WRITING THIS TEXT

Writing a book has always been my passion, from an early age, I wanted to express myself through writing, from a Farm in rural Mississippi to the big city of Jackson, Mississippi and from Jackson to Portland, Oregon. There has always been an urge to

Write what's on my mind and in my heart. The text would be written from the heart and through the experiences that I have witnessed or became part off, talking to creditable people, both relatives and friends, things I have read about, radio and television.

The reason for writing this particular text is to shed the light on how far we have come, but it also shows us how far we have yet to go in achieving full rights and citizenship in our nation. Many people's eyes were open during this "History-Making Event" in our nation.

Good to see people out to vote, for many, this was the first time that they had ever cast a vote and really took an interest in the political system, be it local or our national elections.

Black President was the greatest motivator in getting people out to vote, people saw hope.

Many times I had an urge to write about something or someone, writing had to be factual and not fiction, after my retirement, I had much time to write my first book, I had it published and was a success among friends and family. For those who read the book in its entirety, were satisfied in what they had read. I wanted people to try to understand what was in my heart and the urge to write about my experiences and the laws that minorities had to live under in our nation. This was another motivator for me to write.

Tribute to my parents, to relatives and friends who did not live long enough to see the first Black President in our history, this was something that they had only dreamt of.

Many of the people in the past were strong believers in the Holy Scriptures and tried to live their lives in hope, faith, and belief that change would come. Paving the way for change to come to their love ones and to their people, God never forsakes His people.

They were strong people, they trusted in the word of God, although many didn't live to see the dream manifest, God was true in answering their requests and their desires.

Leaving a legacy for children and grandchildren, in searching for truth in our being in this country, I found that many of our people can only account for three or four generations, however, we know that our history in this country goes way beyond those generations, reasons being slavery, dismantle of all our history, our man-hood, human existence, the language was taken away, children sold to the highest bidder, wife or mate was taken from husband

and children. Women used for slave-masters conveniences and those same slave-masters profess to be God Fearing Christians and believers in the Holy Scriptures.

The hardest thing about writing a book is to have something that you can and want to write about if you have things already on your heart that you want to write about, then telling the story would be easy. Many of us have much that we can put into writing and share our thoughts and experiences with others, if this is your desire and you have information to write a text, then you should follow your heart and share your information with others.

AUTHOR: James Leon Bryant Jr.

PLACE OF BIRTH: Wesson, Mississippi

PARENTS: James Bryant Sr.

MARITAL STATUS: Married

SIBLINGS: Four

OFF SPRINGS: Four

Born in rural southern Mississippi, the town of Wesson then moved to Jackson, Mississippi, living there until my thirteenth birthday then moving west to Portland, Oregon where my father planted his roots. Friends and relatives were left behind, and it was one of the saddest things to do, memories of these people will forever be on my mind, we had a true love for each family that we knew, and respect for all that we didn't know. Southern hospitality was given to all, strangers, relatives and good friends all received a warm welcome. Laws in the south kept the races from expressing their love towards each other.

Civil War is still being waged, although the physical war has been over for more than 150 plus years, the psychological and mental war is still being fought, we still have those die-hard prisoners of war refusing to give up. Through generations of being brain-washed and told that they are superior to those that they enslaved, the war must continue until all reminisce of the old war is gone. Bad feelings and all evils must be eradicated through education, communication, associations, and live the true "Christian Life" they claim to have.

Information that is gathered and contained in this text, consists of experience, talking to creditable friends and relatives, listening to talk shows on the radio, and watching television, reading newspapers and other literature, if the literature is creditable, it helps to confirm my writing this text. Never in Presidential History has any Candidate been under this much scrutiny and criticism, never has it been so much opposition to his proposals. He never wavered from the proposals that he presented to Congress, the more his proposals were opposed, the stronger in the eyes of the voters he became. Right over-wrong I became even more interested in writing about the political process that we live under.

From a Presidential Candidate to a first-term President, his journey was intentionally obstructed by the opposition party and their critics. Anything that they could criticize him on was done. Accusing him of not being one of us, that he's not an American, he is not a Christian and he was a Kenyan, he hated White Folks and did not share their values.

Trying to understand why this kind of campaigning is allowed to exist in our society.

The world is watching us, how we act and do our business has an effect on what they think of our system of government. A better light should be shown to the world on how we live.

INTRODUCTION OF OUR TWO TERM PRESIDENT

Barack Obama, the first Black President of the United States of America, has proven that in his very first term as President, he was qualified for a second term. Public opinions prove to win out against the opposition. Never in America's History has a President been under so much scrutiny as this young President, yet he stood fast and firm on things that he believed would help our Country come out of the recession that we were experiencing.

Born in America to a Black Kenyan Father and a White American Mother, this triggered additional hate and resentment from the opposition party and their critics, this was too much power to put in the hands of a Black man, up from slavery to become king was not on the opposition's list of powerful people, being strong and intelligent proved his case.

Despite the negativity coming from the opposition party and their critics, he got the votes.

Building upon his success from the first term, some things were left unsettled, now with his second term things probably will be easier to get passed. The opposition party and their critics had tried nearly everything in their books of dirty politics to try to defame and dissuade him from being successful for his second term. His first term record proves his achievements and qualifications for a second term, the opposition party was beaten at their own game, some things that took place in the opposition party should be illegal, things that were said should not be allowed to be part of their campaigning strategy, yet the grand old party is responsible for the divided country that we live in, and a contributor

Too much of the violence that takes place in our country daily, their racist attitudes toward minorities, their hatred of poor people, and their unconcern for the elderly and disabled.

Our nation and the world watched as our campaigning and election process took the full circle, what they gathered from what they saw will be a determining factor on how we are looked upon as a Christian Nation, if we are going to sell democracy around the world

Then we need to let a bright light shine so other nations can see it. We still have too many Old rules and policies that the grand ole party is trying to hold on to, they refuse to accept change and will do anything to suppress the Black and Minority votes. Truth is, the grand ole party has existed too long, this is where the real change needs to take place and the rich ole party has been in power much too long. This is a new time and new people that will replace the Jim Crow era, these new people consists of people around the globe, coming to America to search for the "American Dream" people of all backgrounds and races will be the instrument of change. No longer will it be Black and White, it will be people against an unjust system and replacing those that have been in powerful positions too long.

Young Whites, both male and female will help spearhead the change that is coming to our country, Blacks, Hispanics, Asians, Native Americans, and many other groups will form a voting coalition to put who they think is the best representative for the country.

And their interest, for five hundred years, these old policies, laws, and rules have kept us in an enslavement environment; people were intentionally held back from achieving and getting ahead, while these old and powerful people were increasing their margin between those that had the "American Dream" and those that are seeking a better life.

SECOND TERM PRESIDENT SPURS HATE AND RESENTMENT

Soon after the re-election of the first term President, hatred and resentment presented its ugly head, they wanted people to know that nothing has changed towards race relations and they would show their racist hatred whenever the opportunity presents it, these were people that had been brain-washed by their ancestors and the older generations, they are taught to keep the old way of life alive and to never give in to change, always look upon minorities as being less than them, they believe that all power was given to them by God.

And minorities have nothing to say in the power making decisions. One of the main reasons for these die-hard racists not to change their ways, is many in their society have specific people to keep fanning the flames of hatred, these people are not seeking peace nor do they want harmony among the races or other minority groups, these people are angry because they lost the Civil War and cannot let that go, they want to blame Blacks and other minorities for their lack of material wealth, money and the undesirable conditions that they find themselves in, it's easy to blame the powerless for bad conditions.

Clean President that ran a clean campaign, and who won his office clean, yet at every chance the opposition searches for lies and cheap shots to throw at the President; this is their way of trying to win the White House. Never has it been so much money put into the Presidential Campaign by the opposition to defeat a two terms President as did this. The election process, there were tens of millions of dollars spent by the super contributors.

Mostly went to the opposition party. Advertisements and other presentations to demean and discredit the President. Although the negativity, Falsifying continued throughout his first term, he never wavered from his messages. The opposition party was determined to make him a one-term President; they used any means necessary to accomplish their goal.

They played the race card, saying that he was the food stamp and free stuff President.

Many things were passed during the first term of his Presidency; many other proposals were denied, it wasn't because they were bad proposals, but this was another way that the opposition party used in denying him a second term. Intelligent voters soon saw what the opposition party was trying to do and denied their plea to discredit him, for a short period of time, the opposition thought they had a voter's surge going, this happened shortly after the President's first debate, the President was a very good debater, but he did not try to perform to the extent that the voters had expected him to perform. Many of his supporters wanted him to be more aggressive toward the challenger, and to be more challenging on things that he had proposed but was defeated on, obstructions the reason for not passing.

Among some of his proposals that were passed or agreed to pass, health care, loans for students, immigration, pay equity for women, bringing troops home from all wars and national security, bringing terrorists to justice, eliminated Osama Ben Laden, another top terrorist leaders, and their followers. Most of these people were killed or captured. There are more to be brought to justice, in time, they will be brought to account for their terrorist activities. This is a summary of his accomplishments during his first term.

TRUTH ABOUT OUR POLITICAL SYSTEM

Our Political System and racism, seldom mention through our news media, but there is much racism inside our political system. I have listened to the radio and watched television for many years, I became interested when Obama became a legitimate candidate for our President, my enthusiasm grew from that point on, the more he was accepted and his following continued to increase, the more I became interested. This was the first time that I really thought that a Black Man or any other racial make-up would really have a legitimate chance of being the President, up to that time, my thought about politics wasn't very good, it would be more like business as usual, Whites would be elected as always and the minorities would be left out of the process. There should be more minorities in a diverse neighborhood to be represented in our political process, should be more Senators.

President swore to be a President for all the people, and not for a few rich and wealthy ones, he has tried to live-up to his Commitment, he faced objections and obstructions on nearly all his proposals, the obstructers swore, their number one objective was to make sure that he was a one-term President. Opposition party wanted these most powerful positions to remain under white control, the good ole boys club wanted nothing more than to keep things just as they are, any minority acceptance would be on the lower end of the decision making processes. The opposition party has no progressive agenda to move our country forward, it's easier to continue on the same course laid-out my the older ancestors, they refuse to recognize that times are changing, we have new people with new and better ideas to lead this country into the twenty-first century, no longer is this country an island unto itself, we need all nations to participate in this new world's Economy, the rich and wealthy will have a limited role in how the world turns for the future.

Money and power is losing its grip on how people vote, we now have more educated and intelligent voters than ever before, now engages in our political processes, these new voters are more informed of our past and know what is needed to move our world forward. Nations around the globe are in unison with the new movement toward a better world for all to live, no longer will nations be only concerned about their own welfare,

But the welfare of all nations, young people know that we truly are my brother's keeper, what affects one off our nations will eventually; have an effect on all nations, people are starving and dying each day around the world from starvation, wars, lack of medical care and shelter, most of this suffering can be eliminated, if greed was not at the forefront of our world's agenda. This is what the President hopes to do in his second term.

How can we be a leader in showing the way using a very dim light to light the passway?

We need new batteries in our light in leading the way forward, so the path is bright and clear, with a clear and concise voice, we can plea to others to follow us to a path of accomplishments, love, peace, medical care, food, and a bright future for their children.

We set ourselves in a position of leadership; you lead by living and teaching the correct way to live for a brighter future for all. When greed is eliminated we can accomplish this.

EDUCATED FOR THE FUTURE

Education is definitely the answer to our success in a more educated world, without the proper training for the high skilled jobs of the future; we must educate our people to be ready to meet these new jobs and challenges, this is why the President is advocating this fact, many of the old jobs that our ancestors had taken for granted is gone and will not be back, those that do come back will require a much higher level of education to obtain them, technology has taken over our lives as we once knew it, machines and computers are now the instruments of today, and without the proper education to use the computers we will be left out of the equations. This is the reality of our future, for some in our society that had limited education before the technological era will have to re-train for that same job that they had taken for granted, or train for a totally different kind of a job, this is the way of the future, we can either jump aboard the transition or be left out of the future.

President has been speaking on this matter, with an ever-changing world and competition

With other nations, our young people need to prepare themselves for the future, most of the older people that will loose their jobs could retire earlier than what they had expected or re-train for another occupation, some will be bought out of their jobs earlier than they had expected, but too young to retire altogether, many of the seniors have not reached the age of social security to help supplement their obligations, or prepare for their retirement.

President proposed assistance to those that found they were jobless and had a hard time meeting their obligations, an extension was added to those that had lost their jobs and could not find other employment. President has done much in easing the financial burden on citizens, Medicaid and Medicare is an important issue to seniors, disable and the poor, he also paved the way for children to stay on their parents' insurance until they reach their twenty-sixth birthday, and he also made possible for disabled veterans to receive better care.

Citizens making their wishes known, politics as we knew it, is now the thing of the past and the old way of doing business is no longer acceptable to the voters; voters want to see accountability for what is promise. Our voting block is now made up of a more diverse population, and all groups want to become part of the process. Young people will lead the way for a better tomorrow, people of all persuasions coming together to make their voices heard. Whites, Blacks, Native American, Asians, Hispanic and other groups know that there is power in unity; these groups want basically, the same things out of our Government. Jobs with decent pay so that we will be able to meet our obligations and security for our families, educational opportunities for our children, equal pay for equal work, respecting contributions to the jobs, justice under the law and a unified government, these are some of the issues that voters are concerned with, in addition to social security and our medical affordability, taking nothing Granite, we must pursue our dreams with an education and learning new skills. Our young people are not left with choices; it's a must that they prepare themselves for current jobs, and jobs of the future.

Attending trade schools to learn how to use their hands-on skills more efficiently and positions require higher education for jobs in the future.

WARS GOBBLE-UP OUR FINANCES

Wars are very expensive to fight, only the war-mongers would starve its' people and fight wars that they could not afford to fight. Rich nations waste money on wars that not necessary to fight, many times those that are more powerful than the nation that they wage war on, like to exercise their military might, power, and dominance over other nations. Less powerful nations are subjected to harassment, threats, sanctions, boycotts and other tools used to force a less powerful country to comply with the more powerful wishes. Trillions of dollars are spent each year by wars and tools of wars, other nations prosper from these wars through the military hard-ware that they make and sell to the warring nations. Poor and less powerful are left scratching to survive. Our President is trying to bring this fact before the world's audience, much of the suffering and killing can be eliminated if these unnecessary wars would cease, there would be more food and other help for all, greed and the quest for power is the main reason for the world's problems.

A good man that expresses love for all of mankind, President has made it known his concern for the poor and the powerless in our nation and in the world in which we live.

His fight has always been about the elderly, poor, disabled, youth and minorities that don't have power in the world. President understands God created the world that we live in and all the necessary things for all his creatures to live and survive on, there's plenty for all to partake in, from the greatest to the least of all creatures, God has supplied our needs for survival on this planet in which he has placed us, yet there are some that think this planet was created only for them, from the creatures in the sea to the fowls in the sky away has been established for their survival and all their offspring's, man is the only creature that has a mind to think, a heart of kindness and love, and compassionate toward all God's creation, the man was given the authority to rule over and to be good stewards over other forms of life, plants, water, seeds to grow our food, fish, and meats for food.

Many men only want to live as wealthy as they can, and forget about those who are less fortunate than them, when the President spoke of the disabled, elderly, poor and minorities he tried to open the eyes of many people, so they could see the disproportioned of wealth among our people, education on what we can do to narrow this disparity on our planet and elevate the standard of living for most families, when a man has a job that pays well he is happy, his family is happy, and society as a whole will be better off. Less crime and less imprisonment, less taxes to house the prisoners, and educational skills that will make them feel like being part of our society. Under our present system, prisons are a revolving door for many, it's a money-making situation for others, we can do better in helping others to overcome this repetitious life style and live a life of being wanted and valued.

Never in our history has a President fought so hard to carry-out his agendas, never have we had a President that took his job and his agendas to heart as this President does, his emotions, and visible expression in relating to his audiences, people can see his sincerity in what he says, he really cares for others, he really tried to get all things passed that he had promised the voters, but the opposition party would continually obstruct and would not work with the President, this party is the reason why things are the way that it is now.

COMMUNITIES, FAMILIES, CHURCHES, SCHOOLS

All have a responsibility in making a better country to live in, it starts at home with the parents, making their children lives better than the life that they had experienced when they were children, this is a new day and the opportunities to do better is here for your children that were not available for you when you were a child. The parent should encourage their children all that they can to achieve. Create a good environment for their children to be proud of, teach them about life the outside of the home and what is required of them to succeed in a competitive world. Take heed in what the teachers are trying to teach them, be obedient and well-disciplined in school and paying attention to classwork.

Where there is only one parent in the home, communities, churches, schools and other youth organizations should be a mentor for some of the troubled students, there are times when it does take a whole village to raise a child, other times it only takes the right teacher.

This President has lived the life that many of the young people are experiencing now, he came from a one-parent family, and his father left his family and went back to Kenya, leaving his mother to care for him alone. However, his grandparents fill the void that his father had left behind. President said he was a troubled youth growing up, he had a White mother and an African father from Kenya, his father was an educated man that received his education in the United States, left and went back to Kenya, his mother and grandparents cared for him growing up. His mother left the mainland and moved to Hawaii and from there to other Asian countries, he got to see people and how they live in other lands, he was coming of age with on-hands experiences, communications, compassion, and love.

Spiritual guidance is the most important thing in a man's life, God created us to worship and to Glorify Him, without his guidance we will continue to have problems in our life.

We were created to worship God, if we fail to let Him guide our lives, we are doomed for failure. President know about Spiritual Guidance, he has come from a long way back and without this guidance, he would not have come this far. He is a gift to mankind.

A man was chosen to lead this country by God and his every step in this process is from God, despite the opposing party negativity toward him, a way was made for him to be successful in this position, I believe this President has a mission to fulfill, Hands of God is upon him and his every move is being guided by the Holy Spirit, I believe this was the right time for God to present unto the world someone different, an intelligent person with the blood of two races of people, he is half black/half white, this mixture of blood make him more acceptable to the majority in our country, and most of the nations of the world.

Whosoever God places in key positions, no man can deny him, he will remain to carry out his mission, and after the mission is complete we don't know what lies ahead for him.

God sets up leaders in Government and He brings down leaders in Government, having the leadership of nations is God's will, and if these leaders don't do what is expected of them, He will bring them down and replace them with someone of his choosing, God want strong and just leaders' people that will be guided by the Holy Spirit of God.

BUYING OUR POLITICAL LEADERS

Money is a good thing to have, but money cannot buy everything, it cannot buy the true spirit of discernment, the truth between right and wrong, good and evil, money is only a tool to be used in the correct way, not as a tool of deception, lies, distortions, murder, greed, buying positions in our political system and other evils that come with the power of money, it's only a medium of exchange for materialistic and physical goods, not to buy leadership or position in our political system. This type of a system is geared towards those that have money or have access to getting money; this type of system will never be a just system, it doesn't tell us who is the best and the most qualified person for the position in which they seek, voters receive a dishonest candidate for that position, more money spent on a candidate; usually will determine the out-come off an election, the best person for the position is left out of the process under these conditions.

Restrictions on how much money is given to our political candidates, elections should not be determined by how much money is thrown into the process but in the sincerity and heart of the candidate. Our past elections have been money dependant, those with the most money to feed on lies, distortions, deception, and negative television ads ruled the day, not to say that the best person was chosen for the position, but voters were swayed by the amount of money that the candidates spent. Thank God, this is no longer the case.

Voters are now more educated on our the political process, they are more informed now than ever before, they are not being brain-washed in believing any and everything that money bought candidates say and who is behind these candidates with large sums of money, awareness, fact-checking, character, past record, good vetting process and spiritual guidance is the criteria for choosing the right candidate for the position in which they seek. This President has been purged, tried, through the fires of hell, still he remains in office. $1,000,000,000 was the most expensive Presidential Campaign in our history never has so much money been put into the campaign as the election of 2012-13, the opposition party pumped the largest share into this election, their monies came from super-contributors that put millions of dollars into the campaign to try and defeat the President, there were no limits on what they would do to defeat the President and keep him from having a second term as President, this was a ridiculous move made by the opposition.

They thought this would be business as usual, they had told their supporters that they were ahead in nearly all categories of concern and they were assured of a victory for the Presidency. They lied to their supporters, giving them a false hope on winning the White House. After all the dirty tricks that had been played by the opposition and all the money that they had spent, their trickery and lies at the end had let them down. Accusations in their party had begun; groups within their party began to blame each other for losing.

A testament to right and wrong, we know that wrong will survive for a short time, then evil will be over-taken by good and right, evil had run it course, now good and right has taken over, voters were shown the correct way to vote, led by their hearts, not money.

VETERANS AND THE DISABLE

Citizens that answered the call from our Government to go off to fight wars on foreign soil should be given top priority on jobs, food, shelter and medical attention, for some, they will never come back, and other injuries, many suffer psychologically, families of these brave men and women deserve much better than what we have given them.

Many will never be able to work on a regular job, many have lost sights, legs, arms and been mentally challenged. Our Government owes these veterans the best that a country can offer them. Lives lost to protect our way of living, sacrifice given so that we may remain free and to live the "American Dream" businesses and other corporations should make room in their establishments to hire those Veterans that are seeking employment and are physically able to work, it was they who made possible for them to own business, homes, jobs, and liberties to travel back and forth through-out this Hugh country of ours, many of our people have disabilities from birth or received their disability later in their lives, these people should also be given special attention, before their injury, they were contributors to society, how can this party dismiss or not count these people as being part of our society? These people only think of themselves, not who helped them get in the position that they hold, they act if though they are entitled to be in the decision making positions and looking down from the top on the ones that are down below them.

The opposition party will stop at nothing in regaining power and control of these top positions. Why do people in the top financial positions seek these power making positions? They have more money than they will ever need, yet they seek more money, power, and prestige, why don't they just fade away into the sunset and let a much younger group take control, people with skills to communicate and compassion for others.

The opposition party cannot accept they lost the election to a Black Man, they were sure that they would win the election and their candidate would be our next President when all the votes were in and the winner was this Black Man, all hell began to break out, the opposition party is fighting among themselves, blaming one another for the loss. Then began to blame the President for buying the minority votes, accusing him of giving the minorities gifts and free stuff, President won the election fair and square with people coming to his plea of changing the way business has been done in past elections, he told the voters the truth about the situation of the country, he also told them what his intentions were if he was elected for a second term. Unlike the candidate for the opposition party, he knew the direction that he wanted the country to travel in, and what it would take to achieve it.

Despite lies, deception, criticism and other negative advertisements, it all was fruitless in the end, the voters had spoken and chose their candidate, and he was the right one for the job.

Consistent in his messages, never flip-flopping on his ideas, and sticking to his agendas and convincing voters that he was the man for this job, besides, he had proven himself in the first four years of his Presidency, the opposition candidate didn't have the knowledge of being a President. However, he received recognition as a businessman and a one term governor, this alone did not qualify him to be President of this great nation.

TRUTH BEING REVEALED

Despite the perception of what we think of our country, the facts will bear witness to the truth. To fully understand the situation in our country, we first have to find out where we came from, what kind of mindset did we have arriving here? Why did we leave the country that we were into the search for a new land? Whom did they find on the land that they called their own? What was the intent of the settlers toward the native people after arriving on their shores? How were the settlers greeted and how did they respond to the kindness that was shown to them by the native people? What kind of governing and political skills did they bring from their homeland to this new land that they would call their own? After arriving on these shores, what were some of the first things on their agendas and what kind of respect did they give the natives in this land, wars that were waged against them to possess their land? Settlers brought the same kind of mentality with them to these shores. When they became more comfortable with their surroundings they then began to take whatever they wanted, this mentality goes on today in our country.

Corruption has been a major part in our survival in this country, if we were to eliminate all the corruption that is taking place in our society, we would cease to exist as a great and wealthiest nation on the face of the earth. Truth sometimes hurt, but it will be the one thing that will set your mind free, no longer will you have to live a lie, living under make-believe false- pretenses. Although some good things have come out off this way of living

For some and for others it has been negatived in their lives. There are people in our society that struggle daily in trying to sustain food and shelter for their families, this type of lifestyle is why settlers left their homeland, kindness and appreciation should be given to the native people for their generosity in accepting them on their shore and not plotting on how they would over-take the native people and possess their land, native people were slaughtered and nearly wiped out for their land, only to be placed on reservations that were controlled by our government, this has been the way of the settlers.

Blacks brought to these shores through slavery, their manhood, womanhood, records of any history, children sold off, and many other things were stripped from them, and they were brought to these shores to serve the settlers, work their fields and build their homes at no cost to the settlers. The settlers got settle into a new way of life on someone else's land, as more settlers from Europe began to come to these shores, so did the expansion of territory, wars against the native people continued. Many wars had been fought over someone else's territory and up-rooting people off their native lands, many died from starvation, diseases, murders, and other atrocities, why aren't the whole truth taught in our educational system? Is it because we refuse to accept the truth and rather believe a lie? Or is it because a lie sounds better to our ears? Regardless of what the reason for not wanting to accept the truth, the facts remain the same, you can only hide the truth for so long then it will eventually manifest itself, we should take a serious look at the reality of it all, we cannot change what has happened in our history, but we can accept the truth.

This is why we have corruption and other evils surviving in our society, I repeat what was said by creditable sources; "if all corruption were eliminated, we would fold-over"

PRESIDENT AND THE RIGHT COURSE

Voters approved on the course that the President is trying to take our country in, still, the opposition party refuse to come aboard and support his agendas, they see a man with a mission and did not want him to receive any credit for anything that would give him popularity with the voters. Old politics are dying out along with the people that practice it.

New and young people will be the rulers of our future, we will have more diversity in our political making process, of course, this is something that the opposition party hates, they don't want change for the better, they rather keep things just as they are and have been for the last four or five hundred years doing what they choose, whomever they choose to do it too. President is trying to change this old and prejudicial way of leading this country, he can relate to all people that will listen to his plans, the majority will listen to his plans, but we still have those die-hearts that would rather do just that then to make any changes. Progress cannot be stopped indefinitely; sooner or later it will manifest itself.

When the leaders of our country are doing the correct thing for the citizens that they represent, we should let them know by being behind them and encouraging them in any way that they can, this is a testament that he is doing the correct thing, although they are doing for the voters what had been promised, we all need a little pat on the back now and then, this helps to re-enforce their commitment to the people that they have sworn to serve.

Leaders will never get everyone to agree with the correct way things should be done, but if the majority of the peoples understand the sincerity in making promises to them and leaders are trying to carry-out those promises, this is a good indication that they will do what they say. Hard job in being President, when the world is in turmoil, people look to the President to have influence in correcting the situation, our president has a big role to play in the world's affairs, in addition to the domestic problems, sometimes it seems unfair for us to over-burden our President with many of our local problems.

States that can be trusted to be fair and just with the citizens of that state, should exercise their responsibilities in coming to the aid of their citizens, but some of our states not trustworthy in providing justice, equality, and Opportunities for many of its citizens.

If all power were back to the states, it would be like it was in the '20s '30s '40s 50's and even unto this day in many of our states, it would be business as usual, minorities will be discriminated against and unjustifiable arrests convicting them and sending them off to prisons, once they receive a prison and conviction sentence, they are maimed for life little cooperation will hire a convicted criminal, and when he is released from prison he faces an uphill battle in society, with no means of support, eventually, ends up back in prison. Cycle of imprisonment is nothing but a revolving door, it is designed to keep the prisons full, regardless of how minor these criminal acts are, and they are designed to elevate the crime to a prison sentence. Many are making money from the penal system. By keeping the prisons full and supplying the supplies and other necessities for prisoners.

Taxpayers are constantly paying the tab to keep the prisons going, but a few are making t profits from this scheme; this is where our Federal Government is needed.

FEDERAL GOVERNMENT TO OVER-SEE STATES

Our Federal Government has a very important role to play in the lives of its people and without it, minorities and the disadvantaged would continue to suffer under states' rule; states would always favor those that had the most money and power in our communities, this has been past practices from most states, the fact is, we would not have come this far with integration, equality, and justice if it had not been for our Federal Government. There has been divided by the southern states and the federal governments before the civil war, most off these states are still angry over losing the war to the federal Government or the union army, southerners saw their way of life being taken away from them, free labor, freedom for slaves, equal rights, integration, slaves learning to read and write, land ownership, freedom of religion, and dare to dream of a better tomorrow for all, southerners could only see one way to live; this was the way that they had lived for many years, they have always had things their way, they fought and died to keep it their way.

Many people on both sides of the divided nation died, through the years more died in exercising their rights and the rights for others to have a better life. Although this was a Black and White issue, many other people died in fighting for a just cause for all people.

Professed to be Christians would never deny the God-given rights of any human being of being free and to achieve a better life for their families, but we were dealing with people who had greed, jealousness, hate and other evil intentions on their minds. We can still see some of the remnants of those old Jim Crow laws today; we see it in our politics, schools, and churches, this infestation of hate has plagued this nation for centuries and it is hard for some to come to grips with a changing world. During this process of change, there still will be those that have been brainwashed into keeping things the way they were.

Old ways die hard, but progress is slow and sure, right will rule over evil for the future and the leadership will be younger and a more diverse group of leaders.

Many will not embrace this kind of change, there will be some of the younger people succumb to the brain-washing done by their ancestors and there will be some that don't trust young and diverse leadership with that much power to lead the greatest nation on earth, and there will be others that will resist change because of their selfishness and greed. This movement is taking over around the globe; those that are seeking a better world for all to live in will rule the future. There will be food for the hungry, peace where there are war, communication, and dialogue where there are isolation and cast-a ways. We all will have a part to play in the world that we live in, we all will have the responsibility to become good stewards over the things that were put before us, from the environmental impact to the medicines that we consume, the energy that is used to run factories and other pertinent operations. This is what the President has fought hard for, changes in the way that we do business and to do it more efficiently, all this is possible with cooperation.

The requirement of all hands aboard will make many of our dreams come true, we live to see a more equable change to take place, and at the end of this transition we will feel

Good About our achievements, we can pick and choose who we want to lead us in the near future. Money should not determine who our leaders should be, it's an obstruction.

WHY THE REPUBLICANS ARE CALLED OBSTRUCTIONISTS

There are many reasons why this political party was given this name, the name truly fits their deeds and thoughts, they believe only one way, and this is for them to have all power over everyone and everything. They believe only the white people in this country should reap the bounty that this country has to offer, and preferably the southern whites.

They believe minorities have no rights and should not be in a power-sharing position.

They especially believe blacks should be back in the fields and servitude jobs and not in a position of authority. These are centuries-old thinking handed down from generation to generation, goes back for at least four or five hundred years, this mindset won't allow them to progress, to share politically or materially. They have had a yoke around the Black Race for centuries and they don't want to loosen the tension of the yoke.

How can these people live in a country of diversity and not want to share in partaking of this country's riches. I wish there was a nicer or a more sophisticated word to use, but this seems to be the best one to fit these actions. Evil is the word that is used to describe this kind of action by these people, they forget all about the people that helped build this country with their suffering, sweat, and blood, displacement of families, selling humans as if they were livestock, killing our men and raping our women at will, the character of these people is manifested each day, somewhere in our country, someone is denied justice and equality, a decent living and the right to provide for their family, yes the evil deeds and how they think tells much about this political body. They don't want changes for the betterment of everyone, keeping the power in a select few, and those who have monetary

Clout, this is what they live for daily. President is trying to break this yoke of suppression.

Many have given their lives to maintain this way of living, many that gave their lives for a cause that wasn't justified, they were fed lies and told other untruths about the situation of our country about to be attacked by other countries, many of our citizens volunteered to fight off the aggressions that they were told that were happening to our country, good citizens bought the propaganda and volunteered their services to help fight the aggressors. Many of these wars were started by the obstructionist party; many were drafted into service to go to war and never returned. These dedicated citizens gave their lives to defend mostly lies. Many times we fought wars, we provoked the other nation into war, few wars that we fought had been fought justified; many have been a power struggle, greed, and monetary gains. Why are there few rich people children sent to the front lines in battle? Why do they remain behind the lines or in a position of safety?

To whom much is given, much is expected, the rich should be eager to fight for what they have, but it is much easier to send poor and less fortunate people into battle than it is to send a rich man's son or daughter into harm's way, they consider the poor and minorities are expendable and it's no great loss if they never return home. As bad as it might sounds.

It is the truth. This is the way of the obstructionist; they don't want minorities to learn what's going on inside the power machine? Diplomacy in many of the cases could have been used, instead of making war and encouraging peace, obstructionist prefers war.

PROBLEM SOLVING IS OUR BUSINESS

Problem-solving is all of our business, working together on one accord; we can make a difference in the lives of our citizens. Having compassion for those that are less fortunate than we are, is a good start, understanding their condition and helping in any way that we can to uplift their standard of living, we can contribute by giving food and clothing, shelter, teaching, finance and our kindness. Many of us are only a paycheck away from being in the same predicament our self, this can happen to anyone, at any time in our life, so be kind to those that are looked down on because of their financial status, least educated, and the disabled. All the President's accomplishments are not told in this short text, his accomplishments will continue after this short segment is written about his visions and agendas. He is a man with a mission from God and no man can stop his progress coming forward after his mission is complete, only God knows what his agenda will be at that point in his life, again, young people will be the rulers of our destiny.

From a community organizer, senator and on to become the President of the Greatest country on earth, he has proven his capabilities of handling leadership roles, he is a man of compassion, knowledge, and most importantly, a man led by God. He had enough love in his heart for all people, regardless of the road-blocks and the obstruction that was put before him; he overcame these obstacles and proceeded with the mission that was given him by a Higher Power. There would be no turning him back, the more obstacles that he faced, the stronger he became. All should be happy to see a person other than one of the good old boys be elected for President. Doors are now open; anyone that inspires to this High and Prestigious Position and have qualifications will be given the opportunity to become a candidate. Before the barriers were eased, anyone other than one-off the good-old-boys had no chance of becoming the President of this great nation. Many purposes were filled during this "History-making event" this was a proud time to be an American.

Many nations around the world were happy to see a minority elected for leadership in the greatest nation on earth! None off this would have been possible without the hearts and minds be changed by a "Higher Power" and we know where that power came from.

The situation around the world, and in our the nation had gotten so bad that people were ready to make a change in how business was done in our world, people wanted better cooperation between other nations, more justice, and equality at home, new laws created and some of the old laws eradicated, this truly was a time of change by all nations. We wanted peace instead of preparing for war, diplomacy used instead of sanctions, and power to all nations. There are many things that are still on the agenda yet to be passed and voted on, but his persistence to get these things through congress never ceased. This is the kind of President that the world needs, someone that has lived the life of the over-looked and rejected in our society, the poor and less educated, disabled, the elder and the youth.

Voters have made their needs known through the ballot box; this was the democratic way of making change in our society. Each person listens to the truth and votes for what's right.

TWO SIDES TO EVERY STORY

Being fair to both sides of our Dilemma, the situation in our society was caused by man and we have the power to change that which is wrong and make right, greed and selfishness is the main obstacle in our society, for some, the more that they get, the more that they want to take. These people never seem to have enough of anything. They become selfish and greedy; they would deny others to upgrade their standard of living and to achieve a better way of life for their families. From the creation of every human being, there was a certain amount of goodness and kindness given to them from birth, this gave humans head –up on right and wrong, we also were given a free choice to choose between what is right in the eyes of God, and what is wrong in his sight. He also left laws for our guidance in which to live by, teachers and ministers to preach and teach His Ways. If we choose our free will to follow the Evil One, then we will suffer the consequences that it brings. We and only we have control of the route in which we choose and who we serve.

Making the wrong choice will lead to disruption and everything that contributes to evil doings, this evil spirit has been with man since the Garden of Eden. This evil spirit has been fighting against the will of God, this same evilness is the reason for Satan to be cast from heaven and all his demonic hosts with him, since then he and his host have been roaming through the universe seeking to find something that he can interject himself into.

Remember, his objective is to interfere and disrupt that which God has planned for humans to live by, and to live for. With a Mighty Power that comes from the evil one, there is no way that flesh and blood alone can over-come this satanic force, this will take a much Higher Power than what we are facing to over-come what we confront. God is our only way to victory over this satanic power and without him; we are helpless in trying to defeat this force that tries to take over our lives, with the edge over evils in our world we still are fighting an up-hill battle with the satanic forces in our lives.

We are letting the evil in our politics over-take the rational, reasonable, thoughtful, and compassionate way for us to solve our many problems. We like to think back to the old days in thinking this would be the answer to our problems. The fact is the old days weren't so good either, some of the same problems that they had back then, exists today.

The main reason for having these problems was the hypocrisy that they lived and taught.

Christianity was used in referring to their religious affiliations; this was in words only and did not exist in their everyday lives. This way of thinking and doings have been here for centuries, although some progress has been made, it still has much farther to go to be close to how it was meant for humans to live. Our short-comings have been through greed and selfishness, jealousness and hate, power and dominance, these characteristics all fit satanic descriptions, this is why the most beautiful and powerful Angel was cast down from Heaven, satanic tools of warfare was cast from Heaven with him and his host.

We are not forced to live in the past and live in the sins of our forefathers. They will be judged for what they knew was right at that time, we will be judged for what we know is right in the present time. What we say, what we do, how we live our lives is judged.

PRESIDENT FOR ALL THE PEOPLE

When the President won his first term, his pledge was to be for all the people, not certain groups or races, financial statuses or any other classification of people; he wanted to serve the nation as a whole. The President has tried very hard to get cooperation from his opposition to work with him in passing many of these bills, but the opposition refuses to work with him on behalf of the American People. They don't like the President, mainly because he is a person of another race, they can't stomach anyone else in this leadership position but one off the good old boys. They refuse to accept facts from the voters and continue to oppose what the voters want. The opposition thinks the leadership positions belong to them and they are the ones that are entitled to lead this nation. Times have changed and the opposition has to come aboard. Old ways of doing business are out of our future, new ideas, with young new peoples, will take the lead for a better tomorrow.

This is what the majority of our people want in our leadership; we must help in any way.

Why does the opposition party keep fighting against that which is right in the eyes of God?

With people leaving this world every day to face the unknown, it would make sense to try to do what is right and pleasing in God's sight. They say they are Christians, yet they want to live and believe in doing evil to thy Brethren. Hypocrisy is what we see in this opposition party. This party doesn't want change, they rather continue to live the lives and keep the old policies in place that were set by their forbearers, regardless of the power and financial statuses of this party, soon or later they will have to come to the end of their lives here on this planet. What can they carry with them into the unknown? Nothing that they accumulated here will benefit them on the other side of this life. The only thing that will matter is how their lives were lived on this planet; all the money and power will not benefit them in the end, redemption is their only way out off this mind-set.

With evil all around us, and people dying every day, they still fail to see the life that they live are only temporary and cannot continue on its present course. They are their brother's keeper whether they like this or not, they are responsible to help those that are less fortunate than them, and to help move our people forward to a better life while we are still on this planet. Proving their Christianity would be a good start, and then exercise what they say and believe in the name of Christianity. Why do they think that 2, percent of our population should rule ninety-eight percent of the population? Why would they want to keep poor people poor and all minorities' powerless? Why don't they want to share the wealth and bounty in this country with others? well, the question can summed-up in a few words: greed, selfishness, and a quest for power to rule, these words have been with our people for hundreds of years and this same spirit is with this party today, this

Mentality started from the landing of the pilgrims to our present. Major changes are needed to propel this country and many other nations to a brighter future for all citizens.

Having compassion for less fortunate people around the world and giving them the opportunity to succeed, will minimize the poor, hungry, disabled and elderly on our planet if only the rich would be willing to sacrifice a little more of their wealth.

RESPONSIBILITIES OF THE LESS FORTUNATE

The first thing is for the less fortunate to have the opportunity to achieve; this will come through education, will power, justice, spiritual belief. With the system that we now have, it is geared toward incarceration of the poor and less educated, building more jails and prisons. These institutions cost the taxpayers lots off money to keep these people locked up. There are many that are profiteering from these institutions. Many are occupying space in these institutions un-justly for less criminal offenses. Many off our prisons are run by private concerns that state authorized to profit from taxpayers. However, we know that there are some that should be in prison, many are threats to the citizens in our society and should be off the streets. Many off these incarcerated individuals are in prison for having three strikes against them, they just seem not to avoid getting into trouble and end up back in prisons. There are some that could not find a job, before and after they had served time in a penal institution. Many gave up looking for employment because they could not be hired because of their prison records. They soon go back to prison or jails.

Many people when given the opportunity to succeed will take full advantage of the opportunity to lift their standard of living. There are some that will never take advantage of the opportunities that have presented to them; they seem to be happy with just getting by.

Regardless of those that will not take advantage of these opportunities, the chance to live a progressive lifestyle should be available to everyone. Remember the Holy Scriptures concerning the poor. Many reasons for people to be poor, some are left to the individual, and some are poor because of circumstances beyond their control, many are taken advantage off by policies and criminal activities. There are those that make fair wages, but who aren't good stewards of the money that they earn. Many squander away their money through gambling, buying things that not a priority in their lives and trying to keep up with the Joneses. All these things contribute to having more poor people than necessary in our society. Learning to manage our finances is of most importance to us.

This is not intended to minimize the things that are beyond our control, but there are many things that we can do to live a better life. We know there are crooks and other criminals in our society ready to pounce on anyone that seems less educated and venerable to their attacks and deceptions. There is no place in our society for these vultures that would prey on the weak, disabled, elderly, young and the poor in our society.

Many have worked hard to acquire the "American Dream" but unjust circumstances have dictated the way we live our lives in an unjust society. Education is the only tool that we have to fight these injustices. Many people suffer from a lack of knowledge in our society, they fail to open their eyes to see the real solution to our problems. Many would rather pretend that these injustices, poorly educated, and a complete lack of knowledge don't exist in our country. If we continue to believe this, then the crooks in society has us where they want us to be. Believing that things are what they are, and there is no better tomorrow, making believes that they are living at the top of their dreams. Discrimination and other forms of injustices reinforce their desires and intent to continue to do business as usual, there is no incentive for them to make any changes.

THINGS ARE SLOW
BUT CHANGING

We have been in this predicament for a long time and it will take a long time to make changes in the way we do business. President Obama, our first Black President has lived the life that many are experiencing in their everyday lives, he has seen the disabled not receiving medical attention as they should, much is because of the financial expense that is involved in having medical coverage. Elderly and the young are also left out of the medical coverage, again the ability to pay for the cost is the primary reason for not having medical insurance. None in our society should have to be without medical coverage, this is a necessity in a society where accidents and sickness could strike anyone at any time. President Obama has been fighting for improvements in our medical system since his first term as President, he will continue to fight this battle throughout his second term as President, and this is what he had campaigned on during his run for the Oval-Office. This medical problem could have been solved if only the opposition would work with him. These people seem to oppose anything that he presents before them to vote on.

Education for our young people is too expensive for many. This is another fight that He has been fighting since his first term as President if we are to be the leader in the free world, and then we must make institutions of higher learning affordable for our young leaders of tomorrow. The opposition objects to make it more affordable for some of our brightest young people to receive discounts on their school budget. Only those that are from rich and wealthy families would be accepted in schools of higher learning, and the less financially able ones would be left out of the leadership positions in our country.

Hard to understand these people, they talk one way, and vote in another way, do these people really want to see this country go forward? Or do they want things to go backward? They would like to take us back three hundred years if they could get away with it. Remaining in power and defeating Obama is their primary goal in trying to defeat Him at any cost was their battle strategy, trying to make him look bad on issues.

President Obama has been attacked from all sides of his agendas, religious affiliation, and not being an American Citizen. Of course, none of this was true, but it didn't stop the opposition from trying to belittle and discredit him. No other President has gone through this much ridicule, deception, lies, and hated by his opposition as this young Black Man has gone through. African Heritage was the biggest reason why they gave him so much trouble in trying to get his agendas approved. The opposition didn't care how well the agendas were put together or how good the reasoning was, the opposition would vote against his proposals. Hate was displayed in most of these instances. Discredit this Black Man in any way that they could. Obama, a man with a mission from God and no man can deny that which He Anoints. Storms and the gates of hell may come against that which is anointed, but this cannot knock him off his mission. Even his enemies saw they couldn't win, and they soon had to work with him instead of fighting against him. There is no way that they could win this war; God is in his corner, anointed him for this time in our lives to pave a new course in our Country's direction. Nations around the world approved.

EXPOSING EVIL, AND WORKING FOR A BETTER TOMORROW

Exposure of all the corrupt things in our society is now taking place. We have been blind for too long towards the evils in our society, now the veils are off and we have begun to see things as they really are, and have been far too long. Young people are opening the eyes of our elderly, our less educated, disable, young, poor whites and minorities to what has been happening in our country. Why are there inequalities in a land of plenty? Why do we have selfishness and greed? Most of these characteristics have been with these people throughout their life, many have been taught to be selfish and greedy and that everyone is for self, grab what you can, from whomever you can. This has been the mentality of many that are willing to take what they want and leave others in a state of need. They also will take advantage of others whenever they see an opportunity to do so.

They are not their brother's keeper, they despise the words and work hard not to adhere to it. Only one thing that will satisfy their lust for power and riches, and that is more riches.

President is bringing injustices to light, this is one reason why the opposition to his agendas is being rejected by the opposing party as much and as long as they can, they don't want him to shine a light on things that could have been better for our people in the past, people with this mentality will never completely be satisfied, they will continue to disrupt a normal process of governing. Power and authority is their interest, and not the concern of the needy until they are stopped at the voting booth it will be business as usual with the same old discrimination against the needy at the voting booth, things can be different by voting these individuals out of office. Our votes are the only weapon that we have in reversing this trend. Obama's election for a second term is a good example of how important our votes are. When there is a vote for a certain issue by the public, then we have a voice in which we elect to represent our interest in many issues.

Of course, there are many issues that we don't have a voice in, some are appointed positions and many of the decisions are made by people in these appointed positions.

Supreme court justices that are appointed for life is one example of how our limitations are on what is passed, the laws that affects our way of life, what's legal and new laws made to combat that which is not legal. We need Federal intervention to make sure states are caring for its citizens in a fair and just way. Many states have stood by while their citizens have been discriminated against, not only in public works but also in private concerns, this is another reason the opposition wants limited Federal intervention in states' affairs and many off our states would allow these types of injustices to exist indefinitely, and there wouldn't be anyone to over-see their actions. Voters elected these Governors and they have a responsibility to all the people, not just the wealthy and the Prestigious in our society. President of any party took the oath of being for all people in our Country and not a hand-picked few. Our Federal Government is needed in ways.

Our existence as the world's leader for freedom and justice, security and defense of our the democratic way of life, President Obama, is trying to preserve this way of life.

GRADING OF OUR FIRST BLACK PRESIDENT

We expected the first Black President would be graded on an hourly basis and all the criticism that would follow by those who just don't like him for one reason or another.

There are those that like him and voted to keep him in office for the next four years, his first four years was a success. Regardless of what the opposition thought of him and his agendas, voters thought of him differently, they voted to put him in office the first term and voted to keep him in office for a second term. His messaging and agendas appealed to the voters once again. President Obama is a people's President, he is for all people.

Truthfulness, compassion, diplomatic inter-actions could be seen by voters and nations around the world that he would be the best person to lead the free world and the example of how democracy should be exercised, not only by words but the example set forth by his leadership. President Obama is trying to be that shining beckon for democracy for other nations to see and to benefit from watching this country through our actions.

There is no doubt that we are living in the greatest country on the planet, but we still have many things that we have fallen short off, there are some things that we know about and are trying to correct, and there are other things that we have less interest in correcting.

We realize that every citizen will not agree with a change in our country's direction, but if the majority agrees with the direction in the way the country is going, then we have to continue on this course, for it is our citizens that we want to be comfortable and happy.

We must live like we are a Christian Nation and believe that God has greater things for this country to achieve. Satan is fighting hard against us achieving this goal, but he will lose in the near future. Evil is being disassembled. Satan is working overtime in trying to keep from losing his grip on humanity, he wants confusion, disagreement and a complete collapse of the laws and structure that God has placed before us. Satan is up against a war that he knows that he can't win, but yet, he still tries to influence any and everyone that he can. His only mission on earth is: deceptions, kill, rob, steal and destroy all things that are good.

Opposition Party has played into the desires of Satan, they have proven that they survive on chaos, corruption, disagreements, confusion, selfishness, wars and all evil that will disrupt anything that stands for right and moral, hypocoristic ideas is what they practice and sells to the public. Many will accept this poison and become brainwashed in believing what they have to sell is a cure for their warped mindset. It is much easier to win people over to their way of thinking if those that have hate and revenge already instilled into them. They refuse to see any other way except what they have been brain-washed to believe. Satan keeps a grip on their thinking and refuses to let them think of any other way for them to live. Christians that say they are for the right things in our world know what is right, and they try to please God by exercising that which is right in the sight of God. Evil is not in God's plans, this is not what he would have people to do that love Him and His Laws. God's laws are not reversible or to be changed to fit what man desires, they are constant and will remain this way until He judges mankind; there is no short cuts, no negotiations, and no money can change or minimize His Statures.

LEADERSHIP THAT FEARS GOD, AND BE LEAD BY HIS HOLY SPIRIT

Success in a Presidential leadership is led by the Spirit of God, President that rely upon the guidance of God's Holy Spirit will never fail in his duties as a leader of his people.

Those that leave God out of their decision making are doomed to failure. It is He that sets up governments and destroys them when He is not in their decision making. This is the way God set this structure in place at man's creation and nations were formed, so there is no way that establishments can remain successful without God's intervention into man's decision-making process. Christian leaders wouldn't attempt to lead its people without seeking God's approval, they know where the true Power and Guidance come from, it's not from man, but whom man relies upon from God. For centuries, our country has been in a progressive state, we've made gains whenever we have allowed God to lead us and had a Leader that believed in His Guidance, we've always overcome problems that we face.

President Obama has proven to be one-off these leaders that put God first, and to seek His Guidance in leading his people towards a better tomorrow. We can see the exercising of his Spiritual Beliefs in his decision making. President is on the right course and has the right guidance to become one off the most successful Presidents that this country has had.

People who oppose him see history being made before them; this is something that they, the opposing party didn't want to see, young Black Man, accomplishing things that they could not, and would not accomplish. This is why much off his agendas were not passed.

Opposition party couldn't bear to see more accomplishments being made by this President than any of his predecessors; opposition's primary goal is to make sure he would not make them look bad in the eyes of the voters. Many that had gone before him, dragged their feet in trying to get things passed through congress, some never tried and others didn't pursue certain issues. The opposition wanted things to remain as they were.

Voters are behind this second term President, he has shown his ability to work with the opposition and try to get agendas passed, and he has compromised many issues to meet with the opposition in the middle to get agendas passed, but the opposition has refused to meet him half-way in getting anything done. Voters saw what was happening in the debates and wanted no part in what the opposition was trying to do to the Black President, voters had spoken and re-elected the President to another four years to lead and carry out what he had started in his first four years.

Opposition was too sure of them winning the White House the second time around. Hundreds of millions of dollars were spent in trying to defeat the Black President, many lies were told about him, advertisement on television, radio, town hall meetings were nothing but the negativity that spread over the country about him, in their pursuit of trying to un-seat from a second term as President.

In the end, none off this negativity worked for them, for the voters had spoken, and they knew who the best man for the job was. President was put back into the leadership position for another four years. The opposition was heart-broken and wondered where they went wrong. The opposition had done everything that they could do to defeat the President.

This is a time when all races, groups, and classifications pulled together to change how business is done in our Country, when people stick together for right, they will win.

A GREAT COUNTRY TO LIVE IN

Out of all the nations in the world, we have the greatest country of all to live in, although many things need improvement, we still have the material wealth that far exceeds any other nation on the planet. This is a large country with many resources, much farmland to grow food, pastures and farms, land for our livestock, many lakes and rivers to draw food from, yet, we have one of the world's biggest problems, racism and injustices is still a throng in our sides, discrimination seems to be the order of the day, we prey upon the weak and powerless, we classify people by financial status and materialistic wealth.

And position of authority. We feed the world with our abundance of food and extend

Our educational system to people around the world, still, we have come short in caring for many in our own Country. Much of this comes from greed and selfishness, we like to see people beg for bread and become dependant on others for our needs. We like to look down on those that are less fortunate than us, and with this mentality; it makes us feel if though we are more important than the less fortunate people, this gives us a feeling of power and superiority. We like to keep people in a position of control.

We could be a much better country to live in if only we would have more compassion toward those that are trying to achieve a better life for them and their families. Our ancestors worked hard in building this country for all to have a better life in this country and to extend opportunities for those of other nations that want to come here for a better life for their families. With our standard of living, the poorest one of us would be living like queens and kings in other parts of the world. We need to be thankful for what we have in this country. Many people died in protecting our way of life, not knowing what they were going to war for, our nation said it needed them to help, fight and protect our way of life, but they didn't have much of a life for them and their families. The only thing that they fought for was to keep the rich and wealthy in a position that they have enjoyed for centuries. These brave warriors gave their lives in protecting the rich and wealthy.

Coming back home, if they were fortunate enough to return, came back to the same or worst conditions than when they left for war. This is a disgrace to the richest and most prosperous country on the face of the earth, rich and wealthy should be proud to have people such as these to keep them in their position of wealth. Many died and were injured for their cause, not so much for the soldiers, because soldiers who fought the wars came back home to financial ruins. Many lost their homes, jobs were no longer available to them and many had no other income to support their families, those that were injured had a hard time receiving assistance for their families. This should not happen to the brave warriors. Both physical and psychological war had taken its toll on these brave fighting men and women. Did our government let these troops down? Or was it that our government was too overwhelmed to care for these troops. Those at the top off our political system were not affected by the war and the loss of life and limb. Like all wars the rich prospers from having a war, the wealthy become wealthier, and the poor suffers.

And many times they are worst off than before they went to war. There is a petition between the poor and the rich and the opposition party would like to keep it this way.

RESCUING A FALLING COUNTRY

We need rescuing from falling into a trap; we are headed for the point of no return.

Once had standings in the world of nations, but now we have lost our credibility among other nations. Traditional ways of doing things is a big let down to people now living in a modern world. We still want to live by old-outdated laws and traditions that will not give us a razor's edge in the 21st, century, old ways of thinking have been changed for a new tomorrow. Elimination of all injustices, discriminations, inequalities, corruptions and all other forms that not an indication of being a Christian Nation. Our country is sinking fast, and subjected to be swallowed up by these evil forces, now we are allowing all kinds of evil to take place in our country, God is not respected like He and His will are meant to be respected and Honored, there is nothing good that can come out of this acceptance of evil in our country. We have rejected right for the wrong things in the world, our Country has adopted many of these evils that are brought to this Country and we will suffer the consequences of these evils. Many have turned from God and His Holy Words and accepted idolatry and other forms of Anti-Christ worship. Remember our past history.

Too busy chasing money and materials to devote time to the Statues and Laws of God.

Since the creation of man, there has always been a consequence for disobedience, we can see what happen to a disobedient people when they refuse to live as they were created to live.

We have lost sight of what we were created for, and to whom we owe our allegiance.

This will not be allowed to continue much longer, although the patience of God is long and His Mercy is sure, there will come a time when He becomes a consuming fire and destruction will result from it. His patience will not be with man always, He will destroy that which is evil in his sight, regardless of whom practices evil; we need to turn from these evil things in our Country and our world and start to do what's right and moral.

How can the future of our young people be any happier if they don't have good examples set for them to live by? Once again, we are being hypocritical in what we say and do.

Our young people are looking for the truth; they want to see things we preach are true.

A few good people can make a big difference in the way our Country is traveling if only the good people speak out against evil and immorality. It seems no one wants to be involved in teaching a different direction, Holy Scriptures and what God desires for our lives, and many seem to be afraid that repercussions will take place against them or their love ones. Christians cannot be afraid to speak the truth about any issue if they believe in the Scriptures; they cannot remain silent so evil can flourish. We have the power to change the way we live. Through God, we have unlimited power to change our direction of travel. Many are afraid of our jobs and our positions, not wanting to ruffle anyone feathers, but if we refuse to speak out against that which is wrong, we are as guilty as those that commit the evil. We are showing a sign of condoning their actions, and one that commits the acts to take this as your stamp of approval. Not everyone will change their evil ways, but it is our job as Christians to try and show them a different way to live.

Why are we so infatuated with violence? Why doesn't our government pass laws to ban weapons of destruction in our society? Again, too much power and money rule the day.

SATAN USING OUR YOUNG PEOPLE FOR EVIL

Our young people are being taught how to commit crimes in many ways in our society we seem to glamorize violence and feed this evil to our young people, through movies and advertisements, cartoons, drugs, and the acceptance of adults to allow these types of things to take place in our society; we are too involved in chasing a dollar than we are in creating a moral society. If our constitutional rights are out-dated, then we need to amend them so they will apply to our time in history. Too often the constitution is quoted

When certain people in our society reject amending laws relating to our Constitutional rights because it affects the money that is made from some of these rights, weapons are a prime example of the opposition to amend, the right to bear arms. Big money always seems to have their way at the expense of everyone else's opinion. Our government seems to be powerless in enforcing laws that surround the right to bear arms. We are going downhill fast in our Country; violence is on the increase and no respect for authority. This is what happens to a nation that leaves God out of their lives, we are suffering from this violence because of it. Until we put Him back in our lives, it will continue to get worse; people will become afraid to leave their homes in fear of injuries.

Glorifying violence is a national past time in our country, we like to watch television and read books concerning murder, robbery, immorality, and sexual literature that feeds the tender minds of some of our youths. Adults reap the benefit from these obscenities.

We are one of the few countries in the free world that allows firearms to be carried on streets without being in law enforcement or a security role. What's wrong with our society?

Why can't we see the destruction occurring in the Country? We are blinded by what's going on in society, or we don't care about what's taking place. We have a great nation to live in but we have allowed our morals to decay. God has been left out off our lives and Satan is filling the void, drugs, obscenity, murder, disobedience is the order of the day, we only have one choice to regain sanity in our society; this is to put God back into our lives and depend upon him to lead us forward or we will be going over the Spiritual cliff, and this is where Satan wants us to be. Satan works on the minds of many of our young people.

Adults are responsible for most of the evil that is taking place in our society; they pave a way for our young people to travel, if the way is made rough through sin, then our young people will walk a crooked trail, following in the way that has been laid before them. We are responsible for most of the problems that we have today in our society, we even encourages our youth to become out-laws, racketeers, liars, thieves murders and other evils that plague our society. We seem to be growing a demonic generation of humans.

A generation that is fed by the evils that advertisement bring before them, what they have been taught, what they hear and things they see before them. as this book is written, each week there is a mass murder somewhere in our country, mostly committed by young people in our society, most of these murders and assaults are learned from adults who teach them how to become violent and disruptive, this is the way they think will give them recognition and respect in their surroundings, they practice what they been taught.

Only today another mass murder has taken place, this is the second this week.

INNOCENT PEOPLE ARE USUALLY THE VICTIMS

Learning from our past history, preying on the innocent and the weak is nothing new in our country, for four hundred years or more, the weak and helpless have been the recipients of these cowardly acts, it started with the slaughter of the Native People, then to the Slaves that were brought to these shores, these acts are truly the sins of our fathers.

We have now begun to reap some of the bad seeds that we have sown, it took a long time for things that go around to come back to you, this is the law of the harvest, plant bad seeds and you will receive bad fruit. None off this is pleasant to read or to hear, but you cannot hide the truth indefinitely, eventually, the truth will be revealed, dirt under the carpet will be exposed, people that know the truth will accept what is true and have remorse, but to those that don't want to accept it, will look for other excuses to justify what we are witnessing, disclaiming that things of this nature never happened in our Country, and that we are not reaping the products of planting bad seeds, its bad luck.

Everything under the sun is happening for the reason, whether we can see it or not wanting to admit it, there is a reason for things happening, whether this is good or evil. We plant good seeds, we expect a good product, if the seed is bad and without nourishment, we get a bad product. This same principle applies to the spiritual part of man, planting good seeds and nourishment of the plant will produce a good product. We can detect hypocrisy in what we say we want in society, and what we are ready to put into action. An unstable mind cannot be read easily, show that we won't change in the direction that we are going just enforcement of the laws that we now have on the books, and create new laws if necessary for a stable environment, quit playing games with people lives for the sake of a few pennies, there is no amount of money in the world worth the life of any individual.

No matter how some interest groups try to clarify and minimized the sale of weapons, the facts speak for it. Many people in our country are murdered by guns each year, this fact cannot be disputed, yet the weapon manufacture and sale personnel continue to flood our streets with these weapons of destruction, they were made to kill maim and destroy.

Making money is one answer to these weapons allowed to flood our streets, millions of dollars are made through sales of weapons and mass murder of innocent people are usually the victims, we know that without these weapons freely on our streets, fewer people would be killed. However, man has always found some way to commit murder his ability to kill from a distance would be at a minimum, he would have second thoughts to kill someone if he wasn't sure that he could succeed in doing so, guns have made it easier to commit murder. Suspects would be caught before the multiple murders could occur.

We know what the facts are; we refuse to become serious about the issue and allow it to continue. Why is it so important to allow weapons of mass destruction to flourish on our streets and neighborhoods? When certain people in our country are so powerful that they tell our government what laws should be enforced, and new laws created, then it's time to strip the power from these individuals, we are supposed to be a country that is run by the people and for the people and not any particular group or individual. Big money has taken the place of our voters, laws, and statures are here to accommodate big business.

CORRUPTION FROM WITHIN OUR LEADERSHIP

Many of our elected personnel are taking money from private concerns; many are urged to vote for issues or vote against issues, depending on where the money is coming from.

They promised voters that they would be for their concerns, if they are elected to office.

Many times their promises are broken, they vote according to which way the wind blows.

The right is over-looked and the voters become disappointed in their elected officials and this becomes what is popular with their party and those that support the party. Voters usually elect a candidate who they think best represents their interest, but the elected official soon forgets who put them into their positions. Money and prestige have always dictated what laws are passed and whom it benefits. Money dictated the wars that we have fought, the lifestyles that we live, and everything that our lives depend upon, some have been kept away from certain schools, churches, and other institutions and positions because of big money, we have accepted this way of life, and this is a major reason for many to be denied the freedom to excel in our society. Our President is trying to reverse this trend.

Exposing and clean-up our leadership is what the voters want in our political process, and we want a bigger voice in how our lives are manipulated. As great as this Country is, there is much improvement to be made, two and three-century-old laws and constitutions needs amending or eliminated. We cannot continue to live on old ideas, old laws to lead us in a modern and progressive nation. The world is changing, our nation is changing and so should the laws and out-dated constitutions also change. Opposition party doesn't want change, they rather we remain under the same old laws and constitutions that the forefathers put in place centuries ago rather than making changes to our political system. These old laws and constitutions were for that time in our history, not for this time in history. Forefathers could not predict what the future of this country would need to continue to move forward. Centuries ago, these laws and constitutions were written for the newly arrived settlers in this land, it was to protect the settlers, not the slaves and the native people, most other races and groups were considered property or something less than a human being, so these old laws weren't written to protect any other group of people.

President and the voters have made it clear that a change is needed for the times of now.

Voters backed the President in wanting to be for all people, not a select group or any particular race of people, there are many races of people in this country today, no longer white or black and native peoples, there are many other races that we share this land with.

Rights of every human being should be respected and their contributions honored, this is the only way that we all can be included in this "American Dream" other races have earned the opportunity to chase the dream. President is trying to open these doors for those that have been left out for hundreds of years and include all our citizens to share in the bounty that this country has to offer. Other races were used in making this country what it is today, they worked hard in abiding by the laws, and trying to live the dream of what most people in this Country was seeking. Yet, we still have people in our country that cannot accept any other people sharing power or the bounty of this country with others. These are the same groups of people that oppose the change in our country.

CHANGES THAT CANNOT BE STOPPED

Regardless of how much the opposition hates changes, they can't stop a forward movement; they can only be a hinder to the speed of progress, slowing it down at every crossroad and intersection in our progressive move, billions of dollars have been put into stopping progress and equality for all our citizens, but their money and hatred, their selfishness and greed will not stop us from moving forward. Many of this opposition

See the truth about what their party is doing, and decided that they wanted no part in denying others to benefit from this bounty, some have joined in the movement toward a more progressive change in the Country, others have quit their party affiliation altogether, they don't like what their party stands for, but not yet ready to join the party in power, these people want to be on a winning team and see the old ways falling by the wayside. Business, as usual, will no longer be true to those that believed in this ideological way of thinking. The opposition has fought a hard fight, but cannot win over voters to their way of thinking. They are talking to a much more informed people now.

Voters today are much smarter, younger and more in tune with what's around them then the elder voters. Young voters know us must join other nations in moving forward and the only way that they can accomplish this goal is to elect a young and more progressive leadership to lead our country into the future, replacing the older politicians with a more spirited and progressive representation, everyone that is eligible to vote is encouraged to vote. This is the way of a democratic society, not the suppression of voters but to encourage all to exercise their right to choose those that they think will lead this country in the best direction for our future. When people are behind good ideas, and in their leader's corner, many things can be accomplished. The right will eventually rule over wrong and evil. Wrong and old ways will die by the wayside, and the right and new ways will emerge. This way of life has been with man since creation and will continue through our existence on this planet. Satan has been the master planner of evil and sin.

During the month of December, in the first two weeks, we have had two mass killings and countless individual killings. Why do we pre-meditate to carry-out these killings?

Why are there so many evil and mental illness in our society? Why don't we get serious about these killings of other humans? We know that mass killing is carried out by using automatic and assault weapons, yet we refuse to make laws that would ban or curb the sale of these weapons. We are people that are infatuated with violence and weapons of mass destruction. We accumulate as many weapons as we possible can to idolize and show others the calibers and brand of these weapons, we constantly go to the shooting range or in the back-woods to sharpen our skills and we try to impress others of our accumulations of these weapons, selling the idea of how good of a shooter they are.

When these weapons get into the wrong hands, then murder and mass murder is on their mind. Weapons are available to anyone that has money to purchase them, including the mentally unstable, criminal, youth and many of these hate groups. This trend can be stopped, the glorification of crimes in our communities should never be tolerated, yet our government sits idly by and refuses to take these weapons off our streets, why not?

GIVING IN TO BIG COOPERATIONS AND POWER

We have increasingly catered to what big business want from our government, we have allowed these businesses to dictate to our government what to do, when to do it, and who to do it too. President is trying to stop this trend and to give power back to the people; their vote is their tool to change. These businesses will make money off someone else's suffering and death; they seem not to have any compassion in what happenings on our streets and communities, until these cooperation are stripped from the powers that they possess, this trend will continue, murder and mass murder will be on the increase, life will become just another stumbling block for them, something that can be easily eliminated. Value on life is being devalued on a daily basis, its almost like kill at will, we have many copy-cats in our society, each horrific incident, usually, followed by another; it seems if though one is trying to out-kill the other. Many of these perpetrators take their own life after committing such murder, if they die, there is no way they can be brought to justice, weapons such as these off the streets, the killing of innocent people would be at a minimum and mass murder would be practically none existence.

At a shopping center in Oregon, a young man came into the shopping center to carry-out mass murder, he succeeded in killing a couple of people, wounding a few more and then killed himself. One or two days later, a young man had pre-meditated mass murder on his mind, this time a perpetrator entered an Elementary school in Connecticut, killing 26, there were 18 children, ranging in ages from 5 to 10 years of age, there were 8 adults killed in this killing spree, all killed with automatic pistols or assault rifles. These were senseless killings; most of these deaths could have been avoided if weapons off mass destruction was not available to them. These two incidents are only two of many that occur in our society yearly, most are not mention in this text; it would take much time to name all the killings that have taken place in a one year period by the use of automatic gunfire.

There is no doubt that uncontrolled weapons in our society is the largest contributor to violence in our society. Advocates that want more access to these weapons will find every reason that they can lobby against gun control, these people refuse to accept facts.

Guns also embolden those that would ordinarily walk away from the temptation of a confrontation. Having access to weapons make them even more aggressive and not to turn their other cheek, with weapons, a suspect can stand a distance away from his victim and kill from many yards away, he would never have to come in close proximity to the victim or victims. Acts of this nature are usually done by cowards, someone that has hate and want to kill but from a distance, if the suspect had to come close to his victim without these weapons, he probably wouldn't have the heart to go through with it.

Good chance the suspect would be denied his chance to do what his intentions were.

People would subdue him before he could carry out his plans, and he would stand a chance of being killed himself by others. Guns are aiding people to commit murder and mass murders, whether advocates against this agrees or not, facts cannot be denied.

TRUTH WILL EMERGE AND SET US FREE

This text is written to help shed the light on what's really happening in a country that we all love if you want to hear and know the truth about many off our problems, then this text is the one to read. My heart lay heavy in hearing and seeing the many evils that are taking over our beloved Country. There is no joy in not knowing the truth about things that are plaguing our country, only the truth told and evil exposed can we begun to make changes in the way the country is led. My hope that through reading this text, the reader will meditate on things that that are said and search for the truth, confirm what is said in this text and compare these words to what you see and think, writing has been something laid on my heart for many years, since grade school I wanted to express what was on my heart, things that I had witnessed, and creditable information from creditable ancestors and friends. There are things that I wanted to share with others; I wanted people to feel and to see the truth about our past, our present, and what direction we are traveling in.

Enlightens on how our past has dictated the presence, and what we must do for a brighter tomorrow. Criticism of our Country and the people that have power over us, wars fought

And people died unnecessarily, diplomacy and compromise instead of sanctions and blockades, our youth and the parent's responsibilities. This is what I want to bring to light for our people. Many already know what the problems are, but refuse to speak the truth about them, some would rather not tell the truth and believe a lie, because this makes them feel better about our situation, but these lies that are lived will not set them free.

I am a "Believer in the Words of God" and not afraid to confess Him before others.

I have witnessed his Mercy and Saving Grace; I have testimonies of his love for me to this effect, so I know that we are subject to a Higher Power than what we see from man.

I would like for my children and grandchildren to look at this text, far after I have long gone and know what was on my heart when this text was written, I want them to know the truth and continuing in serving their Creator, be good citizens and to help others.

This planet is just a way station for us to gear-up, supply ourselves for the long journey ahead, without these necessary supplies, we cannot continue our journey. My hope is that the truth be known to everyone that will accept it, not to bring hate, but to have love and understanding towards one another. Our ancestors have long been gone, but many tried to pave the correct path that we must travel, each generation should be making progress in becoming a more educated and Spiritual people, we should be moving forward not backward, we should not be satisfied where we are as a people now, we should be moving towards positive change, so we will become a Beacon to the rest of the world.

This text is the seventh that I have written, God has blessed me to write what was on my heart to write from an early age, He has blessed me to gain knowledge to put into words what I have witnessed, experienced, and heard through creditable sources a true factual text. Now that I am up-in age and lived long enough to complete what has been laid on my heart to write. My hope is that some person will benefit from reading this story, some one's life will be changed for the better, only the truth can really set people free.

INDEXES

1-p-par1-2-3, Building upon success, voters make their choice, second term President.

2-p-par1-2-3, qualifications and opposition to election, entitlement to power

3-p-par1-2-3, politics and racism, selfishness and greed

4-p-par1-2-3, education, jobless, medical needs

5-p-par1-2-3, wars, warmongers, disabled and elderly

6-p-par1-2-3, communities, churches, schools, and families

7-p-par1-2-3, money, power, and buying our political process

8-p-par1-2-3, disabled veterans, natural disabilities from birth, poor and elderly

9-p-par1-2-3, corruption, lies and revealing the truth

10-p-par1-2-3, President is on the right course, voters, approval, promises

11-p-par1-2-3, Federal Government to over states, Jim Crow Laws, and injustices

12-p-par1-2-3, obstructionist, entitlement, and hatred for the President

13-p-par1-2-3, the greatest country on earth, nation's approval of the second term

14-p-par1-2-3, two sides to every story, greed, selfishness, and compassion

15-p-par1-2-3, the truth about politics, minorities, and the first Black President

16-p-par1-2-3, taking responsibility, taking advantage of opportunities

17-p-par1-2-3, progress and its pace, sureness and patience

18-p-par1-2-3, exposing evil, working for a better tomorrow, young people will lead

19-p-par1-2-3, grading our first Black President, opposition party, lies and deception

20-p-par1-2-3, God-fearing leadership, looking to a higher power for decisions

21-p-par1-2-3, a great country, allowing evil to gain a foothold, greed, and selfishness

22-p-par1-2-3, a falling country, rescuing, Christians and an educated voter

23-p-par1-2-3, Satan and the use of young people, adult's responsibility, violence

24-p-par1-2-3, weapons on the streets, learning from the past promises for the future

25-p-par1-2-3, corruption in leadership, exposure and clean-up, power of money

26-p-par1-2-3, the movement that cannot be stopped, forward progress, master off evil

27-p-par1-2-3, consequences of sins, living in past history, focuses on the future

28-p-par1-2-3, emerging off the truth, freedom from liars and deceivers

AUTHOR'S BIOGRAPHY

Born in Wesson, Mississippi, on a small farm owned by a plantation, father was a share-cropper and earned the family's keep by working the farms and rendering half of the produce raised on the farm to the plantation owner. Life was rough on the farm, we moved to Jackson, the capital, their father went to work in a steel mill, from there, we moved to Portland, Oregon. This is where father made his stand, his children and grandchildren also made their stand and raised their families. This is where my roots took place, and we are happy in Portland, Oregon.

This photograph of my beloved father, James Bryant sr. has gone to be with the Lord

My beloved mother, a good friend to others, and a devout Christian, She has gone Home

This is a photo of our only sister, and the elder of all the children with her husband

This is my photo taken in earlier years;
I am the elder of three sons, with my beloved wife

This is the second elder son; he passed away at a very young age, now he`s with the Lord

This is the youngest son, and the baby of our
four siblings with his lovely wife Judy

This is the oldest daughter and the elder
child in the family, with her husband

This is my second elder daughter,
the second elder child with her elder daughter

This is a photo of my youngest and third daughter; she is now working with her brother

This is a photo of Thomas, our foster son; he has been with us since a very young age. Thomas is one of our family members and treated as such, we are his family.

This is a photo of my first granddaughter and the first to finish college and go to law school

This is my second elder granddaughter, she is also the second to finish college and on to medical school

This is the baby of all the granddaughters; this is her last year in high school and looking forward to college

Photograph of the house that was shown to my mother
in a vision by God, the vision came true and lived
to see all her children grow and live in this house.
Mother and father had come a long way in getting
their roots started; this house will always remind us
in God`s faithfulness to mother and her family

This is a photograph of our holidays coming together, Christmas, Easter, thanks giving and new years and twice a month for Bible Class. Mother and Dad are missed.

This is the photo of our only son and the third eldest child, he is our joy!